I0469601

Debt Free America

Debt Free America

Guide to Financial Freedom

Omar K. Sewell

Copyright © 2011 by Omar K. Sewell.

ISBN: Softcover   978-1-4568-4807-1

All rights reserved. No part of this book may be reproduced or transmitted in any form or by any means, electronic or mechanical, including photocopying, recording, or by any information storage and retrieval system, without permission in writing from the copyright owner.

This book was printed in the United States of America.

To order additional copies of this book, contact:
Xlibris Corporation
1-888-795-4274
www.Xlibris.com
Orders@Xlibris.com
78831

CONTENTS

ABOUT THE AUTHOR

Omar K Sewell founded O&S Associates, Inc. in 2005; a Debt Recovery Firm created to provide Financial Institutions and Small Businesses with the means and solution to recover their bad debts. His vast knowledge of the debt recovery industry enabled him to develop a debt recovery system that recovers faster and more effectively than any competitor. At the young age of sixteen, Mr. Sewell started his career in the debt recovery industry, working for various collection agencies. At the age of 21 he started purchasing and recovering his own accounts, he has grown O&S Associates, Inc. into the power-house company they are today.

Offering his solution and services to Governments, Financial Institutions and the Small Business community, he hopes to not to just recover bad debt, but to give the business community a solution to eliminating bad debt. Getting control on past due accounts was never an easy task. O&S Associates, Inc.'s services enables companies to continue with day to day activities, without having to worry about nonpaying customers, and how they may put a halt on a company's growth.

This book with designed to help all Americans struggling with debt. High School & College students starting off on their journey through life; this book will teach, how to manage money, eliminate current debts, and stay debt free. Before you are able to eliminate your debt, you have to first understand what debt is and why Americans are in so much of it. This book is design to elevate the quality of life by teaching the future of our great nation how to eliminate and keep America a debt free nation once again.

According to the US Treasury Department in 2009 household debt was expected to increase $387,812,500,000 each year after. In addition, the number of failing businesses was estimated to increase 17% in the year 2010. Americans must change their bad spending habits; to inshore the future of our great nation is a good one. Debt Free America Guide to Financial Freedom will also give you a little in site into the year 2009 and its devastating events.

2009 was a devastating year for Americans and many countries alike. Stock markets crashed, home lending came to a halt, car manufactures are in need of government help, and job employment is at an all time low, and tens of thousands of Americans are losing their jobs each month.

What do you do? How do you save a nation?

Educate Americans on how to manage money, and give all taxpaying citizens $10,000 towards a new life.

In 2009 President Barack Obama put a massive stimulus package together in hope to stimulate the nation. Many people would like to blame the financial crisis of 2009 on the banking industry, like any business; banks have to generate money to continue their day to day services. Banks generate money through many different ventures; mortgages, student loans, business loans, and credit cards are just a few. With Americans having access to large lines of credit, this can tend to create an air of affluence around them. This is where the bad spending decisions come into play.

When someone receives a credit card in the mail with a $10,000 line of credit the best thing they can do is cut it up. Many Americans were approved for mortgages they don't have the means to pay back or they just mismanaged their funds. With this air of affluence around them, their line of credit will quickly deplete. Usually by this point the person with the debt problem is in so deep that depression complicates the quest for any good solutions. This debt-ridden person must carefully weigh all the options to getting freed from debt.

People don't tend to think about the unexpected things that can happen in life. Owning a home has its own yearly maintenance expenses, as well as owning a car and many other unexpected expenses of life. This is where money management and saving comes into play. There is a resolution to escaping from debt; Americans have to relentlessly pursue this goal until it is reached. Part of this is stopping wasteful habits and overspending.

Overspending or careless spending is much like any other vice, it can become an addictive habit. For some, the personality type of the over spender is one that is concerned that they give everyone around them the impression that they have endless financial resources. These are the people who must buy just the right gift for each family member and friend, even if they cannot afford it. Their fear of being seen as something less persuades them any way. This may also occur because they cannot keep up with the lavish spending styles of others. **The biggest key to freeing yourself from debt is to live within your means!**

For some it takes a terrible financial setback to get them to realize this. Some won't stop overspending until they are in a corner, choosing between eating, taking care the family or buying a gift for someone else. Debt can creep up on you and before you even know it, you're in way over your head. Before you know it your getting one credit card after another, now they're all maxed out.

Also stop buying things on payment plans because you can't afford to pay for them all at once. All this does is give you another bill for something you might not even want once you finally pay it off in 12 months. Remember new technology is marketed every 9 months. Many single parents work three jobs just to pay out their credit cards they maxed out giving their children everything they every wanted. And now they have bad credit, and they don't know what to do.

Debt happens to everybody and for every reason, but admitting that doesn't make a difference. The important thing to do is just simply move forward and to be proactive about your debt. Everyone has debt and everyone can work towards eliminating it. The inability to reduce debt and saving money are the two biggest obstacles preventing Americans from living financially sound lives.

National statistics show that money problems play a role in 80 percent of all divorces. One in 54 households will declare bankruptcy. Debt is at an all-time high, particularly credit card debt. The total amount of consumer debt in the United States is nearly $10 trillion dollars and growing. If you are a typical American family, you have $25,000-$30,000 worth of credit card debt (excluding mortgages, car loans, and student loan payments), and you're paying $500 to $900 every month in endless minimum payments.

For example, if you were to continue making minimum payments on a $9,000 debt, and not add any more debt, it will take you over 10 years to pay it off. You will end up spending many thousands more than the original amount and 80% of the money paid will have gone to interest and fees. Most people add more debts as they go, so the reality is this—**Without an aggressive approach to terminating debt once and for all, you will NEVER get rid of debt.**

Today, people have options. There are four strategies for dealing with problem debt you will see advertised: Debt Consolidation, Consumer Credit Counselling Services (CCC), Bankruptcy, and Debt Negotiation. Each strategy must be considered carefully!

DEBT CONSOLIDATION

The Common Approach

Unfortunately debt consolidation is the most common solution people think of when they fall victim to financial problems. It is a sad fact that about 75% of people who consolidate their debt find themselves in much deeper financial trouble than they were in to begin with. All consolidation loans do is transfer debt from one place to another and is invariably a short term fix with long term pain. A debt consolidation loan will not reduce the amount owed. This is not going to get you out of trouble and most of the time will only make things worse. Again, consolidation is not a plan to get out of debt but is instead just getting new debt to pay off old debt.

Also, if you decided to consolidate, you would need to qualify first. Qualifications include equity in a home or good credit and debt to income ratio. Most people burdened by debt find that even if they wanted to consolidate their debt they couldn't qualify for the loan anyway. Once you have taken out this loan, you have just gone from an unsecured debt to a secured debt—and gambling with all your assets. Consolidation loans are spread out over a 15-30 year period, leaving you exposed to losing your assets over the life of the loan. If you run into further difficulty in the future you stand to lose your home, car, and valuables. The fundamental problem that people run into is that once the debts are paid off by the loan, they discover they have a new line of spending potential: empty credit cards. It's not long after these accounts are cleared that they are run up to the limit once again. This will leave you with both the consolidation loan and maxed out credit cards to repay. How are you going to repay the loan and the credit cards when you were unable to pay the previous debt in the first place? You will find yourselves back in the bank for a second consolidation loan, extending your debt and making your debt problem even worse.

Bear in mind that being in debt leaves you with less cash you need to buy and plan for life's necessities. Although a consolidation loan may give them a lower payment and a little more breathing room, consolidation is not going to leave you with the cash to get you and your family through the next 10 to 30 years.

CONSUMER CREDIT COUNSELLING SERVICES (CCC)

Feeling of False Security

Consumer Credit Counselling Services (CCC) programs have a failure rate of 85%. They simply aren't effective.

Here's why: you meet with a counsellor who analyzes your monthly budget. The counsellor will submit a proposal to your creditors for a reduction in the interest rates. They will then pay a monthly payment to them and they would then distribute that monthly payment to your creditors. These programs generally take 5-7 years to complete. The theory here is that the overall payment per month is lower due to the counsellor's success at obtaining lower interest rates and more favourable terms with the credit card companies and banks. This approach is most often recommended by the banks themselves.

Here are the facts: CCC Services were created in the late 1970's when credit card and loan companies began to notice that many people were having problems making their minimum payments and defaulting on their debt. In short, the so-called "non-profit" companies are owned by the credit card companies and banks! CCC agencies are funded by commission by the credit card companies based on the debt recovered from you, normally around 12-15%. This means that for every $1,000 that you give them, they can take as much as $150. If you are paying them a service fee of $20 per month, and the creditors are paying them $75, you can quickly see that CCC agencies are not working for you but for the creditors.

In addition, they have no insight into what the CCC agency is doing on your behalf and no control over the repayment process. You send in your single monthly payment, with no idea of how much is going to which creditor. Since most counsellors are busy people who work based on high volume, getting a return phone call can be difficult. It's key to know that with CCC programs, there still paying 100% of the debt plus a lower interest rate. The debt they walk in the CCC with is what you walk out with. With all things considered, it works out to be about the same as your current minimum payments.

BANKRUPTCY

The Last Straw

Today more people than ever are turning to personal bankruptcy as a way of solving their financial problems. Estimates indicate that 2003 saw nearly 1 in 70 Americans filing for bankruptcy. People owing as little as $5,000 are unknowingly filing, not knowing of alternative methods of eliminating their debt. The reason people take this hasty action with such a low debt amount is the harassment and overwhelming pressure from impatient collectors trying to recover their money. In the case of Consumer Credit Counselling agencies, once they find that they are unable or unwilling to help, they will suggest bankruptcy as the answer—unconcerned of the effect it will have on your future.

In bankruptcy, a court order forces all commercial creditors to cease and desist from attempting to collect the debts you owe them. Depending on the bankruptcy declared (Chapter 7 or 13), it stops wage garnishment, reverses judgments, and generally wipes out debt. For some people, bankruptcy is the only sensible option. If they have $60,000 in debts, and they'll never earn more than $1,200 per month, then their broke! The sooner they eliminate the debt, the sooner they'll have a fresh start. With more than 1.4 million bankruptcy filings in 2000, Congress is passing legislation that will make it tougher to declare bankruptcy.

In bankruptcy, certain personal property is treated as exempt. The banks and creditors cannot touch that property in attempting to recover the money owed to them. Their home, car and other personal effects like clothing, and other assets are considered exempt, but this varies from state to state. Any property that is not exempt is liquidated and distributed to the creditors under the supervision of the court. Since most people entering bankruptcy have only exempt property anyway, there's usually nothing left to distribute, so the creditors typically get nothing.

Seems like a good deal? Many people mistakenly see bankruptcy as a good, low cost way to rid themselves of debt. There are other costs associated with bankruptcy that make it a very bad solution for most people. The cost of filing bankruptcy itself is minimal. Depending on what state you live in, you can expect to pay anywhere from $400 on up to $1,600 for the whole process. That's just the beginning. The bankruptcy will stay on your credit report for 10 years—and on your court records for 20 years. The seemingly "low cost" method will cost them dearly as it will follow them for the rest of your life. If they ever apply for a loan, job, apartment or insurance, one of the first questions normally asked is "Have you ever filed for bankruptcy?" And, for the rest of their life, they'll have to answer "Yes."

You might be able to eliminate your debt, but the effects emotionally and the effect on your personal life will last for many years to come. Consider applying for a terrific job after you have filed bankruptcy. These days, employers will run a credit report to determine how they fared financially. This will effect whether the employer will give you that dream job or not. Even if you do get the job and your employer later runs a credit report on you, they will still have to explain the bankruptcy. While employers can't fire you because of a bad credit report, they can certainly limit your future promotions. Future purchases are affected as well; after several years, you may opt to purchase a home. If you're in sufficient shape at that point to qualify for a mortgage, you'll pay a higher interest rate than the average consumer who has never filed for bankruptcy.

Assume you want to purchase a $100,000 house a few years after filing bankruptcy. You make a $10,000 down payment. This will result in applying for an $80,000 mortgage. While your "good credit" neighbour would obtain an interest rate of 4.5%, you would get a rate of 7%. While it seems that the extra 2.5% difference is not bad for having filed bankruptcy in the past, it's what you will pay monthly where you will feel the pinch. That extra 2.5% on a mortgage will increase your monthly payment by $200 per month with the total of your payments reaching more than $70,000 over the 30-year life of the mortgage.

Besides being a devastating blow to your credit, a bankruptcy can also be a very stressful and embarrassing decision to continually have to explain to every potential lender. If you have no choice, then you should proceed, understanding the consequences. However, the majority of people who take this method of debt elimination don't know what they're getting themselves into or the consequences thereafter. They are desperate, and they get talked into filing bankruptcy by the collectors or attorney without understanding the impact on their financial future.

Keep in mind that personal bankruptcies are usually unnecessary as there are better options available. Many people are forced, against their wishes, to file bankruptcy to protect themselves from aggressive creditor tactics or attorney. Ultimately, bankruptcy still means failure to employers and creditors.

DEBT NEGOTIATION

Light at the End of the Tunnel

Few people realize that there is another solution to burdensome debt, an approach that levels the playing field between you and your creditors, without having to go to court. The debt negotiation strategy will put you back on the road to financial freedom and in control of your life again.

The Negotiation Strategy allows you to turn that $25,000 of credit card debt into $12,500 or even as little as $9,000. In most cases, people have debts totalling $8,000 and have successfully saved them thousands while maintaining a reasonable credit rating. With a professional debt negotiator working for you, your debt can be cut in half.

How it works: You know that bankruptcies are at an all-time high and that the chances of recovering outstanding debts worsen as the debt ages. Your company has the opportunity to close your books on a delinquent account by recovering 50 pennies for every dollar owed by the debtor, or take a chance on never recovering a single penny by trying to hold out for the full value. Also realizing that once the debt leaves your bank (usually after six months or so); it will go to a third-party collection agency. The debt recovery statistics show after 3 months you can expect to collect $0.73 on every dollar. However, after 6 months the amount you're likely to collect drops to only 50% and then to only 25% after 1 year. When you look at it this way, recovering 50%-80% now doesn't seem like such a bad deal.

Now you understand why Americans are in debt, but before you free yourself from debt, you

Most first understand what debt is and the different types of debt.

WHAT IS DEBT

Debt is that which is owed; usually referencing assets owed. In the case of assets, debt is a means of using future purchasing power in the present before a summation has been earned. Some companies and corporations use debt as a part of their overall corporate finance strategy.

A debt is created when a creditor agrees to lend a sum of assets to a debtor. In modern society, debt is usually granted with expected repayment; in many cases, plus interest. Historically, debt was responsible for the creation of indentured servants.

A **creditor** is a party (e.g. person, organization, company, or government) that has a claim to the services of a second party. It is a person or institution to whom money is owed. [1] The first party, in general, has provided some property or service to the second party under the assumption (usually enforced by contract) that the second party will return an equivalent property or service. The second party is frequently called a debtor or borrower. The first party is the creditor, which is the lender of property, service or money.

The term creditor is frequently used in the financial world, especially in reference to short term loans, long term bonds, and mortgages. In law, a person who has a money judgment entered in their favor by a court is called a judgment creditor.

The term creditor derives from the notion of credit. In modern America, credit refers to a rating which indicates the likelihood a borrower will pay back his or her loan. In earlier times, credit also referred to reputation or trustworthiness.

A **debtor** is an entity that owes a debt to someone else. The entity may be an individual, a firm, a government, a company or other legal person. The counterparty is called a creditor. When the counterparts of this debt arrangement is a bank, the debtor is more often referred to as a borrower.

Interest is a fee paid on borrowed assets. It is the price paid for the use of borrowed money, or money earned by deposited funds. Assets that are sometimes lent with interest include money, shares, consumer goods through hire purchase, major assets such as aircraft, and even entire factories in finance lease arrangements. The interest is calculated upon the value of the assets in the same manner as upon money. Interest can be thought of as "rent of money". For example, if you want to borrow money from the bank, there is a certain rate you have to pay according to how much you want loaned to you.

Interest is compensation to the lender for forgoing other useful investments that could have been made with the loaned asset. These forgone investments are known as the opportunity cost. Instead of the lender using the assets directly, they are advanced to the borrower. The borrower then enjoys the benefit of using the assets ahead of the effort required to obtain them, while the lender enjoys the benefit of the fee paid by the borrower for the privilege. The amount lent, or the value of the assets lent, is called the principal. This principal value is held by the borrower on credit. Interest is therefore the price of credit, not the price of money as it is commonly believed to be. The percentage of the principal that is paid as a fee (the interest), over a certain period of time, is called the interest rate.

A **bank** is a financial institution licensed by a government. Its primary activities include borrowing and lending money. Many other financial activities were allowed over time. For example banks are important players in financial markets and offer financial services such as investment funds. In some countries such as Germany, banks have historically owned major stakes in industrial corporations while in other countries such as the United States banks are prohibited from owning non-financial companies. In Japan, banks are usually the nexus of a cross-share holding entity known as the zaibatsu. In France, bancassurance is prevalent, as most banks offer insurance services (and now real estate services) to their clients.

The level of government regulation of the banking industry varies widely, with countries such as Iceland, the United Kingdom and the United States having relatively light regulation of the banking sector, and countries such as China having relatively heavier regulation (including stricter regulations regarding the level of reserves).

TYPES OF DEBT

A company uses various kinds of debt to finance its operations. The various types of debt can generally be categorized into: 1) secured and unsecured debt, 2) private and public debt, 3) syndicated and bilateral debt, and 4) other types of debt that display one or more of the characteristics noted above.

A debt obligation is considered secured if creditors have recourse to the assets of the company on a proprietary basis or otherwise ahead of general claims against the company. Unsecured debt comprises financial obligations, where creditors do not have recourse to the assets of the borrower to satisfy their claims.

Private debt comprises bank-loan type obligations, whether senior or mezzanine. Public debt is a general definition covering all financial instruments that are freely tradable on a public exchange or over the counter, with few if any restrictions.

Loan syndication is a risk management tool that allows the lead banks underwriting the debt to reduce their risk and free up lending capacity.

A basic loan is the simplest form of debt. It consists of an agreement to lend a principal sum for a fixed period of time, to be repaid by a certain date. In commercial loans interest, calculated as a percentage of the principal sum per year, will also have to be paid by that date.

In some loans, the amount actually loaned to the debtor is less than the principal sum to be repaid; the additional principal has the same economic effect as a higher interest rate (see point (mortgage)).

A syndicated loan is a loan that is granted to companies that wish to borrow more money than any single lender is prepared to risk in a single loan, usually many millions of dollars. In such a case, a syndicate of banks can each agree to put forward a portion of the principal sum.

A bond is a debt security issued by certain institutions such as companies and governments. A bond entitles the holder to repayment of the principal sum, plus interest. Bonds are issued to investors in a marketplace when an institution wishes to borrow money. Bonds have a fixed lifetime, usually a number of years; with long-term bonds, lasting over 30 years, being less common. At the end of the bond's life the money should be repaid in full. Interest may be added to the end payment, or can be paid in regular installments (known as coupons) during the life of the bond. Bonds may be traded in the bond markets, and are widely used as relatively safe investments in comparison to equity.

FUND BASE

Cash Credit

This is the primary method in which Banks lend money against the security of commodities and debt. It runs like a current account except that the money that can be withdrawn from this account is not restricted to the amount deposited in the account. Instead, the account holder is permitted to withdraw a certain sum called "limit", "credit facility" in excess of the amount deposited in the account. Cash Credits are, in theory, payable on demand. These are, therefore, counter part of demand deposits of the Bank.

Working capital

Firms need cash to pay for all their day-to-day activities. They have to pay wages, pay for raw materials, pay bills and so on. The money available to them to do this is known as the firm's working capital. The main sources of working capital are the current assets as these are the short-term assets that the firm can use to generate cash. However, the firm also has current liabilities and so these have to be taken account of when working out how much working capital a firm has at its disposal.

Working capital is therefore: -WORKING CAPITAL = Current Assets || stock + debtors + cash - Current liabilities Thus working capital is the same as net current assets, and is an important part of the top half of the firm's balance sheet. It is vital to a business to have sufficient working capital to meet all its requirements. Many businesses have gone under, not because they were unprofitable, but because they suffered from shortages of working capital. Working Capital Cycle

Bank Overdraft

The word overdraft means the act of overdrawing from a Bank account. In other words, the account holder withdraws more money from a Bank Account than has been deposited in it. An overdraft occurs when withdrawals from a bank account exceed the available balance which gives the account a negative balance—a person can be said to be "overdrawn".

If there is a prior agreement with the account provider for an overdraft protection plan, and the amount overdrawn is within this authorized overdraft, then interest is normally charged at the agreed rate. If the balance exceeds the agreed terms, then fees may be charged and higher interest rate might apply

Term loan

Term Loan is the counter parts of Fixed Deposits in the Bank. Banks lend money in this mode when the repayment is sought to be made in fixed, pre-determined installments. This type of loan is normally given to the borrowers for acquiring long term assets i.e. assets which will benefit the borrower over a long period (exceeding at least one year). Purchases of plant and machinery, constructing building for factory, setting up new projects fall in this category. Financing for purchase of automobiles, consumer durables, real estate and creation of infra structure also falls in this category. Bill Discounting:—

Bill discounting

Bill discounting is a major activity with some of the smaller Banks. Under this type of lending, Bank takes the bill drawn by borrower on his (borrower's) customer and pays him immediately deducting some amount as discount/commission. The Bank then presents the Bill to the borrower's customer on the due date of the Bill and collects the total amount. If the bill is delayed, the borrower or his customer pays the Bank a pre-determined interest depending upon the terms of transaction.

Project Financing

Project finance is the financing of long-term infrastructure and industrial projects based upon a complex financial structure where project debt and equity are used to finance the project, rather than the balance sheets of project sponsors. Usually, a project financing structure involves a number of equity investors, known as sponsors, as well as a syndicate of banks that provide loans to the operation.

LET'S TALK

Money, what is money? Money is a piece of paper that is used to represent value. People steal, kill, and many other unspeakable things because of "Money". Some get up and go to work, working 40 plus hour weeks to make money, and there are others that kidnap, rob, murder, and lye all in the name of "Money". Why is money so important to people?

Some try to justify the wrong things they do for money by saying, "I have a family that needs food, bills that need to be paid, and I have to put a roof over my head". These are the same people I ask, what would your family do if you were in jail and couldn't provide for your family? What would they do if you were killed? How would they pay for your funeral? Why not live for your family, sacrifice for your family, try showing your family and friends there is a better way.

The things that happen in the world today are all because of money. War, Stealing, Murder, getting up every day and going to work, going to school to get a better paying job. I'm not saying money is a bad thing, but it's what you do with it and for it that makes money what it is. The majority of people act without thinking, instead of thinking it through, they just act or react. Fear and pure laziness create bad actions and reactions. The only fear is the fear of the unknown. If you knew what great possibilities the future holds you would no longer be fearful. Everyone thinks about wanting more, most because someone else has it. Few think about wanting something because it will help make life easier for others.

If you look at a person's life compared to yours you'll find they are doing something you aren't doing or weren't doing to get to where they are at. If you knew what that person was doing to get what they have you would start doing it or would have been doing it too. The reason you aren't or weren't doing it is because of laziness or simply not applying yourself.

Laziness comes in to play, if you are told what to do to get what you want; you are either going to do it or try to find an easier way to get it done. Easier doesn't always mean better. You know what you want and how to get it, but you are too lazy to take the time to do the work it takes to get what it is you want.

Laziness only makes things harder; it slows you down by putting unnecessary optical in your way.

Fear is, not knowing the outcome of something. If you know the outcome there would be nothing to be fearful of. There is the fear of doing something and something happening that you didn't what to happen. There is also fear of doing something and something happening that you want to happen, because you still don't know what is yet to come or you don't know what to do next because you haven't planned for it. There is always a next step. And not knowing what's next is what's so great; if you knew then there would be no point of doing. You do something to get to an end result because the steps along the way make the journey much more exciting and you can appreciate the end result that much more.

Credit, what is credit? Simply explained, credit is all about trust. Creditors trust in their customer to pay them back what they borrow and a little interest for them lending the money. If everyone had good credit there would be no war, stealing, killing, etc. With good credit there's no need to have paper money, because your creditors now trust you to pay them what they are owed. Imagine a world you can go into any business or financial institution and get whatever it is you want.

In life you have the given and the unknown, the given is when you work you make "X" amount of dollars a week. And as long as you budget and manage your money right you will live a prosperous life. The unknown is when you work and make "X" amount of dollars and spend "Y" amount of dollars without budgeting and managing your money, your lift with not knowing "Z", how you're going to pay your bills, how you going to feed your family, and how you're going to pay your rent or mortgage.

You just have to stop being lazy, and do what you have to do you get what you want and get the job done. A wise man once said, if you give your word "keep it", if you make a commitment "honour it", if you take on an obligation "fulfil it". As an American citizen it is your obligation to help America become a Debt Free America once and for all. The only fear is fear of the unknown. Ask yourself this, if someone told you how to manage your money, and show you were you can afford to cut spending and to pay off current debts and once debt free, stay debt free, would you do it? If your answer is "YES" then follow these simple steps and you will elevate and enrich your life, your future, your family's future and the future of the American Nation.

Step 1: Layout Expense
Sep 2: Layout Household Income
Step 3: Cut Miscellaneous Expense & Cut Back Wherever Possible

Step 4: Follow Plan until Debt Free

Step 5: Once "Debt Free" continue to live in your means & save miscellaneous expenses to purchase investments & start enjoying the fruits of your labor.

Money Management

Housing Expenses.	Monthly	Annually
Utilities (electric, gas, water):	$_____ .	$_____ .
Telephone/Internet:		
Home Repairs/Maintenance:		
Household Goods/Furnishings:		
Transportation		
Fuel:		
Auto Repair/Maintenance:		
Parking/Tolls/Bus/Train:		
Personal/Family		
Food/Personal Care Items:		
Clothing:		
Laundry/Dry Cleaning:		
Doctor/Dental/Prescription Drug Expenses:		
Gifts/Charitable Contributions:		
Entertainment		
Cable/Satellite TV:		
Dining Out:		

Movies/Sporting Events:

Babysitter:

Hobbies:

Vacation/Travel

Other Variable Expenses

_____

_____

_____

Total Variable Expenses $_____. $_____.

Budget Organizer

Housing.   Monthly.   Annually.

Mortgage/Rent Payment: $_____. $_____

Property Taxes:

Homeowners/Renters Insurance:

Transportation

Car Payment:

Automobile Insurance:

Parking/Tolls/Bus/Train:

Loans

Credit Card Payments:

Personal Loan Payments:

Personal Insurance

Life Insurance Premiums:

Disability Income Insurance Premiums:

Health Insurance Premiums:

Dental/Vision Insurance Premiums:

Taxes

Federal Income Taxes:

State Income Taxes:

FICA/Self-Employment Taxes:

Personal/Family

Child Care Expenses:

Education/School Expenses (tuition/fees):

Household Help:

Membership/Professional Dues:

Savings/Investments

Personal Savings/Investments:

Education Savings:

Retirement Savings:

Other Fixed Expenses:

_____

_____

_____

Total Fixed Expenses: $_____ $_____

CREDIT REPAIR

When first deciding to change your life and live debt free, you have to first find out how much debt you're in. To do this is simple and free, each you are entitled to a free credit report from the three major credit bureaus (Trans Union, Equifax, and Experian). Visit www.annualcreditreport.com and take the necessary steps, by ordering your credit report you will now have in writing what debts you owe; now you can take the necessary step to becoming debt free.

Step to becoming and living debt free:

Step 1: Order Free Credit Report
Step 2: Organize Budget
Step 3: Money Management
Step 4: Create A Plan (Savings, Spending, Investing)
Step 5: Create A Start And End Date And Stick To The Plan

Once you receive your credit report in the mail, the first thing you should do is to dispute all claims. The theory behind this is, creditors are given a certain period of time to respond to a dispute. If your creditors does not respond in their given time period the claim must be removed from your credit report, also if your debt is over 7 years old it has to be removed. Follow these simple steps to becoming and staying debt free and your life will change dramatically. Thank you for your time, and support, and best of luck on your journey to becoming debt free.

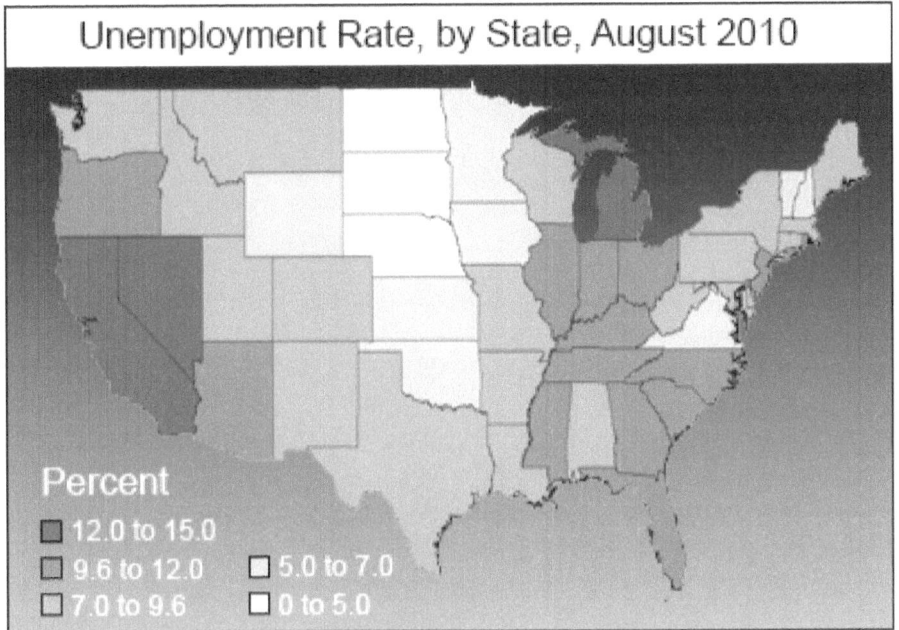

Unemployment Rate, by State, August 2010

Percent
- 12.0 to 15.0
- 9.6 to 12.0
- 7.0 to 9.6
- 5.0 to 7.0
- 0 to 5.0

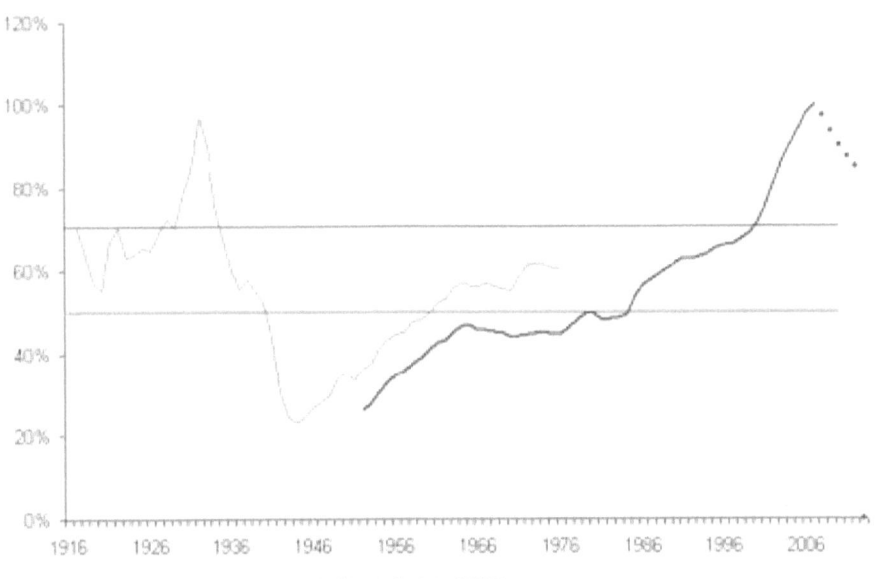

Non-corporate Net Private Debt to GDP Ratio
Household Debt to GDP Ratio (Flow of Funds)
• Possible Scenario

Source Credit Suisse

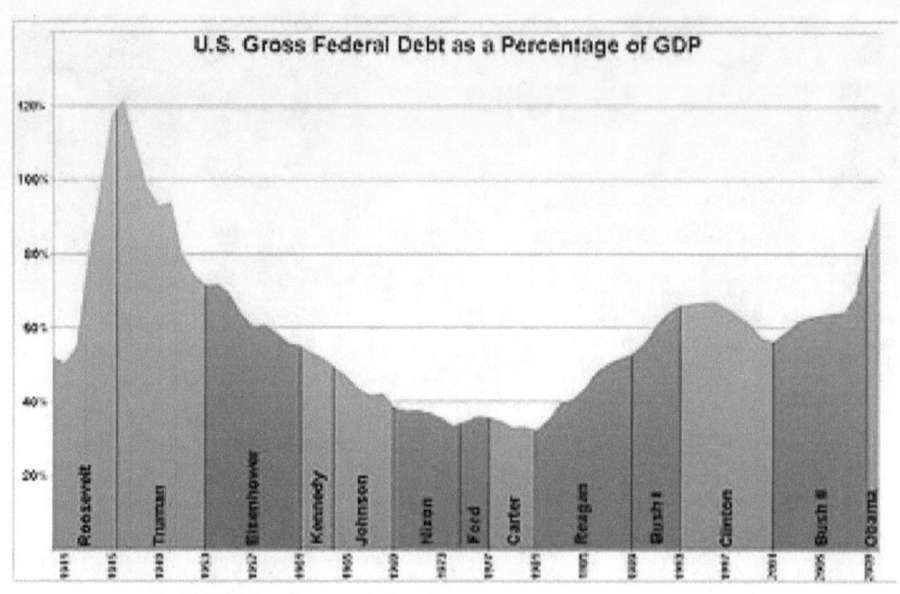

U.S. Gross Federal Debt as a Percentage of GDP

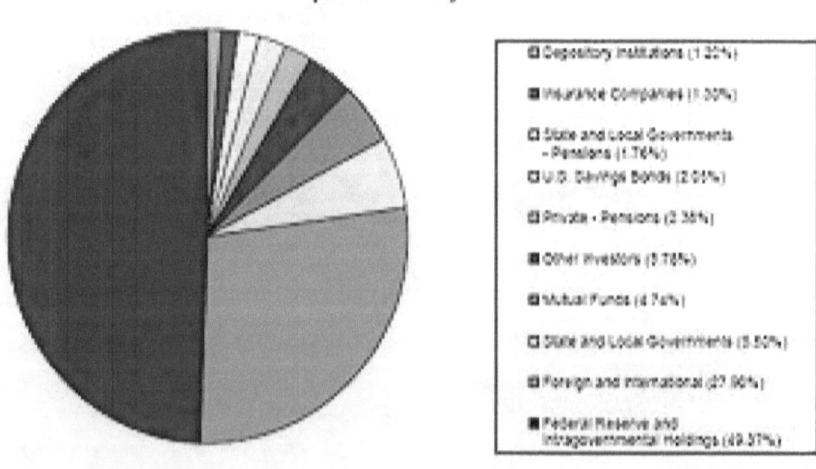

Estimated Ownership of all U.S. Treasury Securities (June 2008)

- Depository Institutions (1.30%)
- Insurance Companies (1.30%)
- State and Local Governments – Pensions (1.76%)
- U.S. Savings Bonds (2.05%)
- Private – Pensions (2.35%)
- Other Investors (3.76%)
- Mutual Funds (4.74%)
- State and Local Governments (5.50%)
- Foreign and International (27.96%)
- Federal Reserve and Intragovernmental Holdings (49.37%)

Revenues, Outlays, and Deficit or Surplus Over the Past Decade

(Billions of dollars)

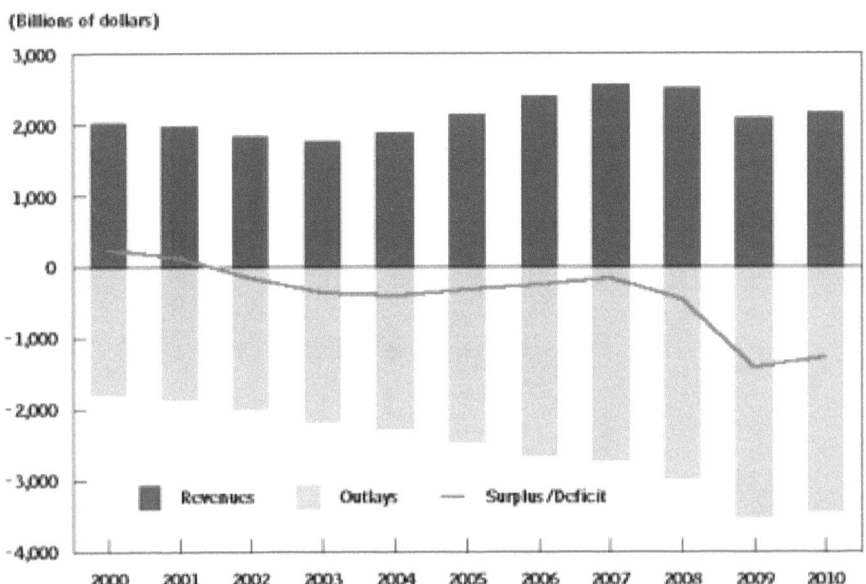

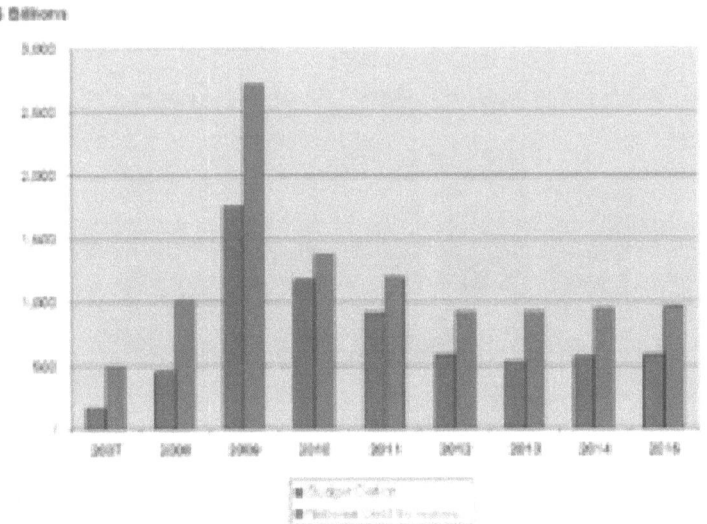

2010 Budget – Projected Deficits and Debt Increases

$ Billions

Total Deficits vs. National Debt Increases ($ Billions)

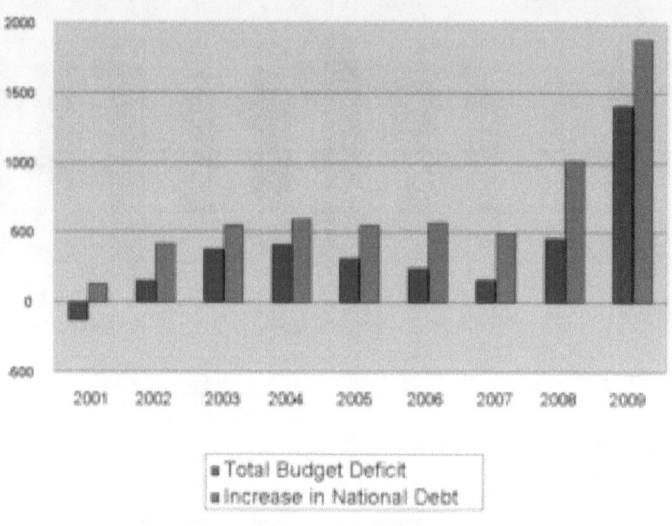

- Total Budget Deficit
- Increase in National Debt

Interest on the National Debt

Figure 2

Total Interest Expense
(in billions)

$355 $404 $433 $454 $381

Fiscal Year Ended September 30

■Held by the Public   ■Intragovernmental Debt Holdings

Source: GAO – Audit of Bureau of Public Debt Schedules of Public Debt – FY 2009

The Risks of Growing Entitlement Spending

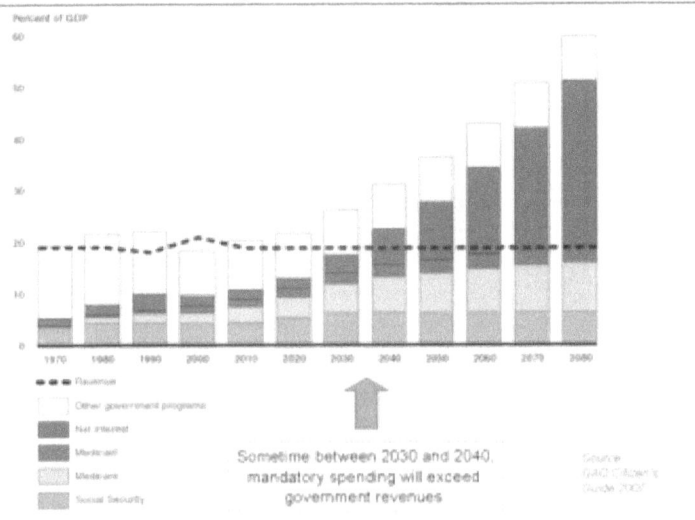

Sometime between 2030 and 2040, mandatory spending will exceed government revenues

Estimated Ownership of Federal Securities

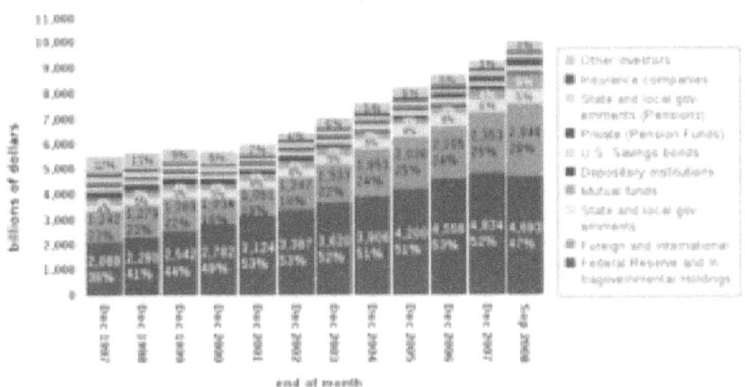

United States Federal Debt (Dec 2008)

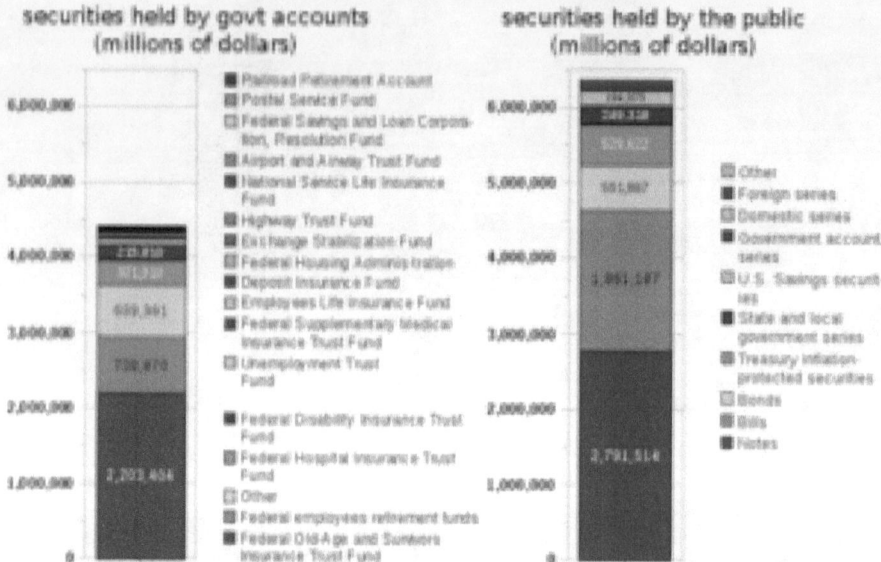

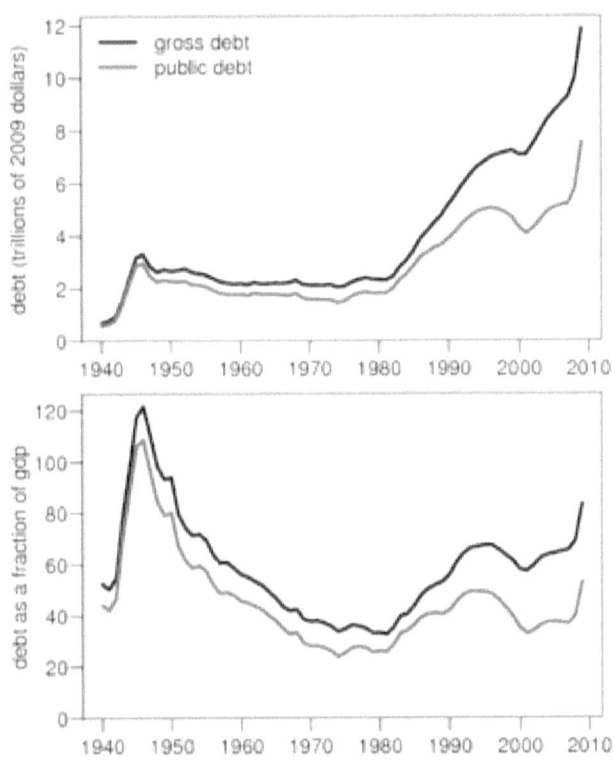

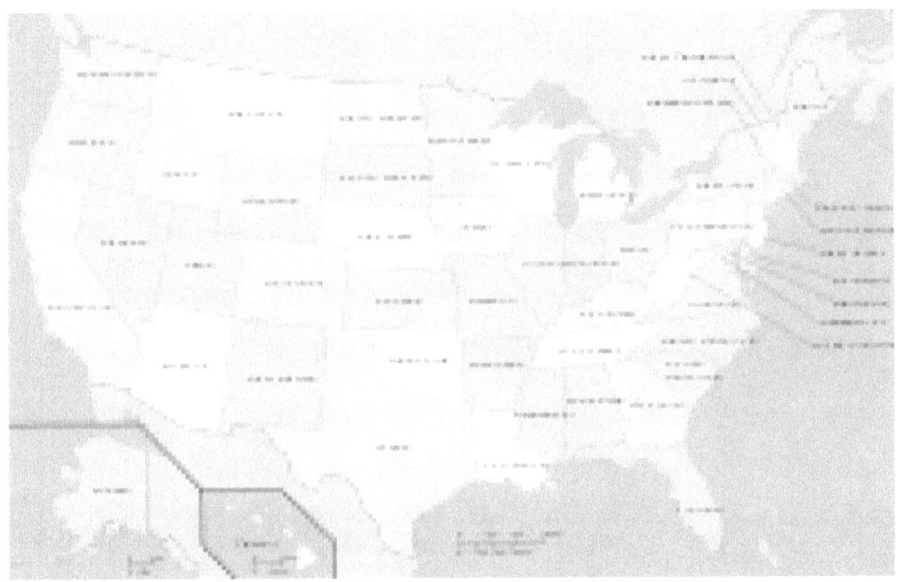

www.ingramcontent.com/pod-product-compliance
Lightning Source LLC
Chambersburg PA
CBHW021928170526
45157CB00005B/2228